Your students can become

roaring lambs

*Helping your high schoolers integrate
their Christian beliefs with real life*

Your students can become

roaring lambs

Helping your high schoolers integrate
their Christian beliefs with real life

Youth Specialties

ZondervanPublishingHouse
Grand Rapids, Michigan

A Division of HarperCollinsPublishers

Roaring Lambs: Helping your high schoolers integrate their Christian beliefs with real life

Copyright © 2000 by Youth Specialties

Youth Specialties Books, 300 S. Pierce St., El Cajon, CA 92020, are published by Zondervan Publishing House, 5300 Patterson Ave. S.E., Grand Rapids, MI 49530.

Library of Congress Cataloging-in-Publication Data

Roaring Lambs : helping your high schoolers integrate their Christian beliefs
with real life.
    p. cm.
    ISBN 0-310-23419-0
    1. Christian education of teenagers. 2. Church work with teenagers. 3. High
school students—Religious life. I. Youth Specialties (Organization)

BV1485 .R63 2000
268'.433—dc21

00-036674

Unless otherwise indicated, all Scripture quotations are taken from the *Holy Bible: New International Version* (North America Edition). Copyright © 1973, 1978, 1984 by International Bible Society. Used by permission of Zondervan Publishing House.

Edited by Crystal Kirgiss
Cover design by Mark Rayburn Design
Interior design by Tom Gulotta

Printed in the United States of America

00 01 02 03 04 05 06 /   / 10 9 8 7 6 5 4 3 2 1

Contents

6 introduction
What is a roaring lamb, anyway?

14 session 1
Bleeding Hearts in Bleating Sheep Inside out or outside in?
Reassuring your students that loving God on the inside is good, but if it's not transformed into outward behavior, they are only bleating sheep instead of roaring lambs.

28 session 2
Welcome to the Ghetto Fighting the battle of Jericho.
Challenging your students to tear down the walls surrounding their exclusively Christian-programmed culture—the Christian ghetto—so they can see the world and the world can see them.

42 session 3
Welcome to the World You're not in Kansas anymore.
Clarifying for your students the difference between being in the world and being of the world.

54 session 4
The Salt of the Earth In praise of a high-sodium diet.
Helping your students recognize their role as the flavoring and preservative of the world.

66 session 5
Careers 101 Will the real Christian please stand up?
Showing your students that pastors and missionaries are not the only ones who can serve God.

80 session 6
Roaring Lambs Step up to the microphone.
Encouraging your students to positively affect the world by living each day for Christ.

What is a roaring lamb, anyway?

L ook around you—at the news, at the media, at the messages delivered over the information superhighway, at the "truths" proclaimed by advertisers. It's depressing. So much of the world is filled with evil, sadness, despair, and a lack of purpose. And all too often it seems like things are beyond the hope of ever getting any better. As the old movie title so aptly states, "It's a mad, mad, mad, mad, mad world." It's also a bad, bad, bad, bad, bad world thanks to sin and its effects.

But there are people who, through supernatural powers, can change that. There are people who, through a direct line of communication to the Creator, can bring about positive effects. There are people who, through their actions and words, can bring a dose of light and truth into the lives of others.

Those people are the Christians, the Christ-followers, the physical reflectors of Christ on earth.

Those people are you and your teenage students.

The question is whether the Christians are actually bringing about change in the world. Are they positively affecting their friends, neighbors, teachers, and coworkers? Are they bringing light and truth into the lives of those around them?

Are they roaring lambs? Or are they just bleating sheep?

In his book *Roaring Lambs*, Bob Briner expresses his opinion that Christians are missing the mark when it comes to how they live their lives. Yes, they are probably trying to follow God's word and to make right decisions. But they are doing it in a closed community, in what he calls the Christian ghetto. He contends that too many Christians live compartmentalized lives. They keep their church life in one box and everything else in another box. They essentially become segregated individuals with all the God stuff on one side and all the non-God stuff on the other.

As a youth minister you need to help your students sort through this issue. For instance, can they really neatly divide their lives into a God-stuff side and a non-God-stuff side? What does it mean to be a compartmentalized Christian, and is it what Jesus had in mind for them when he called them the salt of the earth? Is there a way for them to live out their faith without being pushy, unpleasant, and completely out of touch with reality? The answer to *that* question is yes. Christians *know* that—on the inside. They just don't always *do* that—on the outside.

When they do manage to make their earthly lives and their faith intersect, however, they become roaring lambs—Christians whose faith is lived out in their everyday lives, not by doing little "Jesus things" throughout the day, but by thinking, acting, and living the way Christ would if he were living on earth right now surrounded by school, jobs, movies, television, the Internet, and everything else today's generation deals with.

Traditionally, the church's encouragement to kids has been to live out their faith by injecting the secular with the sacred—to start a Bible study at school, to hang up posters for a Christian concert, or to advertise youth group to a few friends. They've been taught to put Jesus into a turkey baster—to siphon a little bit of him out of their sacred compartment and then squirt him into their secular compartment.

That's not roaring, though. That's bleating. That's saying, "I'm willing to be a Christian as long as it doesn't hurt, doesn't take too much effort, and doesn't draw any embarrassing attention to myself."

Bleating sheep don't change the world. Roaring lambs do.

What the church should be doing instead is encouraging its kids to decompartmentalize their lives, to join the electronics club at school as well as—or *instead of*—the Christian club, to accept an invitation to attend an unbelieving friend's dance recital even if it is on the same night as youth group, or to write a paper on the positive message of Nietzsche rather than a term paper on the evils of evolution.

The church needs to be encouraging students to become integrated, not segregated, individuals. They should *not* be told that the way they serve Christ best is by attending every church youth activity. In fact, maybe some of your students should drop out of the youth choir so they can have time to be in the school musical. Maybe some of your students should step down from the youth leadership team so they can have time to join student council. Maybe some of your students should stop publishing the youth group newsletter so they can have time to write for the school paper. After all, the school musical, the student council, and the school newspaper could all benefit greatly from having talented, committed, Christ-followers in their ranks.

Sixteen-year-old roaring lambs need to live out their faith in study hall, at their part-time jobs, and on their sports teams—*not* just at youth group—because Christianity shouldn't be something they do, it should be *who they are*.

This curriculum challenges high school students to live out their faith in all areas of their lives. The lessons were written to help you teach your high schoolers how to begin the process of decompartmentalizing their faith and integrating themselves as individuals. Hopefully they will start thinking about different ways to turn their Christian beliefs into actions so they can be roaring lambs who positively change the world.

How to use *Roaring Lambs*

This curriculum is based on the book *Roaring Lambs: A Gentle Plan to Radically Change Your World,* by Bob Briner (Zondervan, 1993). This curriculum is not a study guide for *Roaring Lambs*, nor does it cover all the same topics. However, since it includes and explains many similar ideas, it would be beneficial for you to get a copy and read it. No doubt you will be able to use some of the information in it to tailor these lessons to your particular situation.

The following elements will be used throughout each lesson—

Streaming questions

These are to be used as jump-starters for each lesson. Use one or more of the listed questions to get your students thinking about the topic. Just like the Internet's streaming video, the goal here is speed. Do not let your students mull over, discuss, or contemplate their answers. Ask for the first thing that comes to their minds. Let it be a lively affair, not an organized, hand-raising lecture session. Your goal is for them to give you their immediate answers. You may want to have someone writing down their responses on a whiteboard or other clearly visible place for reference throughout the rest of the lesson.

Listen to the music

These activities will be based on lyrics from the *Roaring Lambs* CD. Each activity will have a worksheet for the students to use. The goal is to take one idea from the particular song and think about it as you begin the lesson. **Listen to the Music** will take the students one step further than the **Streaming Questions** by using a medium that most teens immediately identify with—great music.

Getting into it

These are activities you can use with your students as a follow-up to **Listen to the Music**. Several options are provided for each lesson. Choose the one that seems to fit your students' personalities best. Some are active. Some are thoughtful. Be sure to gather whatever materials you will need ahead of time.

The Big Question

This is the main point of each lesson and will resemble the earlier **Streaming Questions**. However, students will probably have some different ideas to offer after having completed a **Getting into It** activity. This is their chance to spend more time thinking about the issue at hand and to discuss it either with their peers in a small group setting or with everyone all together.

Telling stories

An important part of this curriculum is communicating real-life stories of integrated faith with your students. Each lesson includes a story for you to use, but feel free to use your own resources or to bring in a guest speaker for this portion of the lesson. These stories shouldn't be happy, sappy tales. In fact it will be important that they show the reality of life in both its positive and negative senses. The story can be about either an adult or a teen. If you have a student in your group whose story would be appropriate and who would feel comfortable sharing it, use it. If you have a personal experience of your own that would work, great. If you know someone from another church or youth group who has something to offer, go for it. The important thing is that the story be told honestly. No sugarcoating, please. You should not be trying to convince your students that being a roaring lamb is all fun and games with sweet rewards. Keep the story to five minutes or less. If a student will be sharing, have them practice in front of you. If a guest speaker is coming in, ask for a synopsis. If the speaker is willing, provide a few minutes for questions. This is also an appropriate time to use video clips, songs, or poetry that communicate a story fitting the lesson.

Bible

The focus of this part of each lesson will be to see what God's word says about the topic. Students will have had a chance to express their own ideas and opinions. They'll also have had a chance to hear someone else's story. Now they'll get to hear what God has to say and see how that relates to their own lives. If you have kids who typically don't bring a Bible, be sure to have some available. Or pull the text off the Internet (*www.gospelcom.net*) and run off enough copies for everyone to use.

This part of the lesson can be done in several ways. The text can be read and discussed as an entire group. The text can be read as an entire group with the questions being discussed in smaller groups. Or the entire activity can be done in smaller groups. You may also want to consider having students or leaders act out the passage while it's being read. Sometimes *seeing* is more powerful than just *hearing*. If you're going to try this, be sure to prepare your actors in advance.

To-do list

These are worksheets you will give to your students at the end of each lesson. Each one includes an activity the students will do during the week to help them put their faith into practice. Encourage all the students to participate. Remind them to bring the completed worksheet to the next meeting. Always provide time at the beginning of the next lesson to talk about their experiences.

Prayer

Maybe it goes without saying that each lesson should begin and end in prayer. But we'll say it anyway. No one—not your students, not your leadership team, not even you—has any chance of becoming a roaring lamb without relying on God's power. Use this opportunity for more than "Please bless our week and thank you for this time together." Use it as a chance to ask God for wisdom and strength and power to become what he wants you to be and to clearly communicate to your students that positive change, both inside and out, is possible only through God.

Some reminders...

● Read through each lesson at least several days in advance so you have some time to think and pray about it.

● Be sure to have your storytellers lined up ahead of time so they have a chance to prepare.

● Have all the necessary materials gathered beforehand. Be prepared.

● Since these lessons contain more material than can be covered in one meeting, pick and choose what works best for your group. Don't be afraid to alter or mix and match the activities. They are tools for you to use in whatever way seems best for your group.

- Gather your leaders before beginning this series and give them an overview. You may even want to provide copies of *Roaring Lambs* for them to read. They may have some ideas for guest storytellers or for additional activities. Prepare them each week for whatever small group activities or discussions they will be a part of.

- The material in these lessons can be used in several different settings—Sunday school, youth group, or small growth groups. Don't be afraid to use one or two parts of a lesson in one setting and other parts in a different setting.

- When leading a discussion never let your students give simple yes or no answers. Always ask for an explanation. This will encourage and push them to think through the issues for themselves.

- Above all remember this is just a guide. You know your students better than anyone, so follow your instincts about what to use, what to pass over, and what to change.

Bleeding Hearts in Bleating Sheep
Inside out or outside in?

The Big Question [to pose for your students later in the session]

What can you do or what needs to happen in order to make your inward beliefs and your outward behavior similar?

Let's face it—it's hard to be an authentic teen in today's world. In psycho-speak, it's hard to be real. Everyone tells teens to put on a fake front. What matters most is to look good—even if they don't feel good on the inside. And if they don't feel good on the inside, no problem. The world is full of quick fixes that don't really fix anything at all. Feeling sad? Buy something and you'll feel happier. Feeling blue? Lose a few pounds and you'll feel like dancing. Feeling lonely? Dress just like everyone else and watch your number of friends start growing. The world would like teens to think that individuality is what really matters. But the world's real message is that fitting in is what matters most, and the best way to fit in is to dress, act, talk, and be like everyone else.

Many teens are searching for their real identity, trying to figure out who exactly they are. But no one is encouraging them to actually express their individual identities. No one except Christ, that is.

One of the greatest things about being a Christian teen should be the discovery of one's real self. Christian teens should marvel at the fact they are loved unconditionally, cared for, and watched over. Christian teens, though they certainly have their fair share of doubt, identity crises, and other teenage struggles, should be comfortable with who they are deep down in their center—children of God. And they should have the courage to be themselves—to let their *inward* selves show through in their *outward* selves—rather than trying to be like the crowd.

But do they?

Not often. The Christian teens in your youth group probably love Christ deeply, are sincerely grateful for his pres-

> "I am convinced that most Christians have no idea about the possibilities of being lambs that roar—of being followers of God who know how to fully integrate their commitment to Christ into their daily lives."
> Bob Briner, *Roaring Lambs: A Gentle Plan to Radically Change Your World* (Zondervan, 1993).

14

ence in their lives, and truly desire to follow him. In many ways, their hearts bleed for Jesus. But that doesn't always translate into action. While they may be bleeding hearts in love with Christ, they may also be bleating sheep, Christians who haven't yet learned how to synchronize their inward beliefs and their outward behavior. Bleating sheep are a far cry from roaring lambs, Christians who have learned how to live *inside out* so their beliefs are visible to the world.

In C. S. Lewis's book, *The Screwtape Letters*, the junior demon Wormwood loses a major battle when the human prey he's been stalking becomes a Christian. Wormwood's uncle, the senior demon Screwtape, writes—

The great thing is to prevent his [the new Christian] doing anything. As long as he does not convert it into action, it does not matter how much he thinks about this new repentance...Let him do anything but act...The more often he feels without acting, the less he will be able ever to act, and, in the long run, the less he will be able to feel.

How true. The more often teens *don't* speak out for truth, *don't* take a stand for Christ, and *don't* show love to the unlovable, the easier it becomes. We need to remind them that sin is not just doing bad things, but it is also *not doing* the good things they know they should do.

It's easy to be bold in youth group, but what about at school? It's no challenge to stand up for the truth in church, but what about on the job? The challenge in this lesson is for teens to take a realistic look at how they exhibit their faith in the world, and then to walk away without feeling condemned or guilty about past lost opportunities, but excited and hopeful about future opportunities.

Intro
Bleater or roarer?

Explain to your group the gist of the following (or just read it if you want)—

> "Our ambition to become roaring lambs is to more completely serve and obey our Lord who has asked us to be salt and light...you can become a roaring lamb only through the power and strength of the Master."
> Bob Briner, *Roaring Lambs: A Gentle Plan to Radically Change Your World* (Zondervan, 1993).

Over the next six weeks or so, we'll be exploring what it means to be roaring lambs—people who live out their faith in every part of their lives. In this first lesson, we're going to try to be honest with each other about whether or not anyone in the group is really a roaring lamb, or just a bleating sheep—that is, someone who claims to be a Christian but doesn't transfer that claim into everyday action.

You might want to read the C. S. Lewis quote (left) to give students a visual image of what it means to be a bleating sheep and what its consequences are.

Streaming questions

Jump-start your kids' thinking with these questions or questions of your own.

Remember the goal is quick and lively answers.

- **What do your non-Christian friends think Christians are like?**
- **Is there ever a good reason or a good time to deliberately hide your faith?**
- **If people are roaring lambs on the inside but not on the outside, are they hypocrites? Are they even really Christians?**

Listen to the music
Over the Rhine—"Goodbye"

Stuff you need
- On the *Roaring Lambs* music CD, cue up Over the Rhine's song "Goodbye"
- A copy of **"Goodbye"** for each student (page 20)
- Pens or pencils

Introduce this part of the session with words to this effect—

It's often difficult for Christians— or *anyone*, for that matter—to do on the outside those things they believe and know on the inside.

For example, we *know* God wants us to love everyone, we *know* we should honor our parents, we *know* we should only fill our minds with uplifting, positive, and pure things—but we don't always do what we should. In other words, we don't always show outwardly who we really are inwardly.

Hand out **"Goodbye"** (page 20) and play the song for your students. Then let them work on the activity alone, in small groups, or as a whole. Allow time for discussion if desired.

Get into it
The Roaring Lambs Voice Test

Stuff you need
- A copy of the **Roaring Lambs Voice Test** for each student (page 22)
- Pens or pencils

Tell your students they're each going to take the Roaring Lambs Voice Test (page 22) to help them gauge how well they're doing at living out their faith in places other than the church. Encourage them to give honest answers and reassure them that any score is acceptable. Those who score low aren't going to be targeted as loser Christians. Instead they're going to find ways over the next several lessons to move from bleating to roaring.

After students have finished, ask people to share their scores if it seems appropriate. If you have students who will find this too personal or embarrassing, don't push for participation.

...or get into this
I roar / I bleat

Stuff you need
- A copy of **I Roar/I Bleat** for each student (page 24)
- Pens or pencils

Break into small groups of four to six students and hand out **I Roar/I Bleat** (page 24). Explain to your students that *roaring* refers to outward behavior that matches inward beliefs and *bleating* refers to outward behavior that doesn't match inward beliefs. Ask the students to complete each sentence as a group. Someone should record the answers and someone else should act as spokesperson to share the responses with the larger group.

When everyone has finished, talk about this activity using the following questions—

- **Which of the sentences were the hardest to finish? Why?**
- **Why is it more difficult to roar in some circumstances than in others?**
- **Why are outward behaviors and inward beliefs so often in disagreement?**

Now pop it—
The Big Question

Time to cut to the chase and ask the question that everything so far in this session has pointed to.

What can you do or what needs to happen to make your inward beliefs and your outward behavior similar?

Students can answer this question in writing, in small-group discussion, or in the large group.

Telling stories
When behavior and belief part ways

Have someone share a personal story about a time when outward behavior and inward beliefs weren't the same. Remember that the goal of this lesson is to illustrate what life is like when Christians fall short of their roaring potential. The story

you use should reflect that. If you do not have an appropriate story, read the following one to the group.

Sandi, a high school senior, loved music. She'd been in school choirs every year and always did well at the annual district vocal competition. This year she was especially looking forward to Concert Choir because they were going to New York over spring break. Most of her best friends were in the class with her, so it promised to be a great year.

On the first day of school, Sandi sat down in the same chair she'd had for the past two years. She greeted all her friends, laughed as they told their summer horror stories, and joked about how Mrs. Johnson, the choir director, would probably be as unorganized and forgetful as ever. Cheyenne and Megan, her two closest friends, sat on either side of her just like they'd done every year. It never occurred to any of them that things would be different than they'd been before. But when Mrs. Johnson read off the seating chart, Cheyenne had been moved two seats to her left and Megan was in an entirely different row. That wasn't so bad—after all, they saw each other in Study Hall and Advanced Comp. What Sandi couldn't believe was that Mrs. Johnson had put her right next to Becky Gates, a junior who was a total outcast. Becky was intellectually slow—dumb, even. She was anything but attractive. She sang off-key, didn't know how to read music, and never understood what people were laughing at—which was usually something she'd done or said. Becky was everything Sandi wasn't, and even though Sandi was a Christian and knew she was called to love everyone, she couldn't stand Becky.

"Great," Sandi thought. "Just what I need to make my senior year of choir perfect—sharing a folder with Becky Gates. How did this happen to me?"

Over the next few days, Sandi thought about the situation a lot. She realized her attitude toward Becky wasn't what God wanted. She decided that this would be a good opportunity for her to try and live out her faith by being nicer to Becky. She started asking Becky about her classes, how her day was going, and what she'd done on the weekend. For some reason, she assumed that Becky would love the attention. After all, she needed friends, didn't she? No one else in school liked her. In fact, most people avoided her like the plague. So it surprised Sandi when Becky didn't gush over her friendly overtures. After a few weeks of going out of her way to be nice and getting nothing more than a mumble or two in return, Sandi gave it up.

"Hey, I tried," she thought to herself. "If she doesn't appreciate my friendship, then forget it. She can go back to being lonely and unliked." She went to Mrs. Johnson and begged to be moved back by Cheyenne or Megan. Mrs. Johnson

> "Culturally, we are lambs. Meek, lowly, easily dismissed cuddly creatures that are fun to watch but never a threat to the status quo. It's time for those lambs to roar."
> Bob Briner, *Roaring Lambs: A Gentle Plan to Radically Change Your World* (Zondervan, 1993).

finally agreed.

And Becky Gates, the outcast, thought to herself, "Just what I thought...she never really meant any of it at all. She's just like everyone else."

Some things to think about, some questions to explore with your group—

- What things did Sandi do right in this story?

- Why did she give up on doing the right thing?

- What other reasons do people have for either giving up on or avoiding living out their faith?

Bible

The Samaritan roars

Read Luke 10:25-37—the story of the Good

Stuff you need
- Bibles

Samaritan. You may read it to your group, have students read it, or have a few people act it out while you read it. Then discuss the following questions—

- Why do you think the priest and the religious leader avoided helping the injured man?

- Think of a time when you've had the opportunity to do a good thing but have avoided it. Why?

- What made the priest and the religious leader bleating sheep?

- What made the Samaritan a roaring lamb?
- What kind of reward and recognition did the Samaritan get for doing the right thing?

Point out to your students, maybe in words like these, that—

The two people in this episode most likely to be roaring lambs—the priest and the religious leader—were actually nothing more than bleating sheep. Perhaps like the demon Screwtape's ideal Christian, they had spent so many years thinking about what they believed without actually doing anything that they'd finally lost the ability to act the right way.

Yet the Samaritan—a member of a despised country, an object of racial prejudice—was the real roaring lamb. In fact, his actions were so notable that Jesus instructed his listeners to "go and do the same." Not a bad goal: to have

Jesus say that about something you've done.

To-do list

Roaring or bleating? Matching beliefs with behavior

Hand out a copy of **Roaring or Bleating? Matching Beliefs with Behavior** (page 26) to each student. This first *To-do list* (there's one at the end of each session) is easy and basic and can be used by your teens to keep track of their inward beliefs versus outward behavior this week. Encourage them to participate and remind them to bring the completed sheet to the next meeting.

Stuff you need
- A copy of **Roaring or Bleating? Matching Beliefs with Behavior** for each student (page 26)
- Pens or pencils

"If anyone loves me, he will carefully keep my word, and my Father will love him—we'll move right into the neighborhood!"
—Jesus, from John 14, *The Message*"

Listen to the music

Goodbye
Over the Rhine

Help me tell the truth,
You see that's all I'm trying to do is tell the truth
I'm not that shy, this is not goodbye, and later on I won't know how
I don't know who else to be, more and more I'm secretly just me
Open your eyes
Help me tell the truth,
You see that's all I'm trying to do is tell the truth
It's just in my head, all I've left unsaid , and later on it won't come out
I have seen the final curtain fall, if I have to I'll surrender all,
I'm always coming around too late, it's not too latee

So often we know the truth, we believe the truth, and we want to share the truth. But instead, something happens to our good intentions and the truth just stays inside of us. When that happens we are bleating sheep—the opposite of a roaring lamb.

Sometimes we manage to communicate the truth in our words, but our actions don't match up. When that happens we are hypocrites—a characteristic Jesus despised.

Think of a few examples of bleating sheep behavior. Maybe they've happened to you. Maybe they've happened to someone you know. Write them down here.

Think of a few examples of being hypocritical. Maybe they've happened to you. Maybe they've happened to someone you know. Write them down here.

Notice the lyricist's final line—"It's not too late." That's great news for us because it reminds us there's time to grow in our Christian life. Our past mistakes don't have to hold us back or weigh us down. We don't have to be a bleating sheep forever.

Words / Music by Linford Detweiler, Karin Bergquist. © 1999 Scampering Songs Publishing / Cool Puppy / BMG Songs, Inc. (ASCAP)

The Roaring Lambs Voice Test

Circle either Y (yes) or N (no).

Y   N   I have as many close friends outside my youth group as in my youth group.

Y   N   I support decent movies by attending wholesome ones and avoiding unwholesome ones.

Y   N   I have eaten lunch with someone at my school who usually eats alone.

Y   N   I have stayed late at work to help with clean-up even when I wasn't scheduled.

Y   N   I have walked away from a conversation at school because of the negative gossip.

Y   N   I am active in the student council or other student decision-making group at my school.

Y N In class I have volunteered to partner up with the kids everyone else dislikes.

Y N I have shown respect to my boss even when he or she seems to be on my case all the time.

Y N I have talked with at least one non-Christian friend about my relationship with Christ.

Now add up your points. Each "yes" is worth 1.

8-10 Congrats. You're a bona fide roaring lamb.

5-7 Good job. Someone's probably listening to you.

2-4 Your mouth is open, but no sound is coming out.

0-1 Baaaaaaaaaa!

I Roar / I Bleat

When your inward beliefs match your outward behavior, you are roaring. When your inward beliefs don't match your outward behavior, you are bleating. Complete each of the following sentences as honestly as you can.

I roar in my relationship with my parents by—

I bleat in my relationship with my parents by—

I roar at school by—

I bleat at school by—

I roar with my friends by—

I bleat with my friends by—

I roar with new acquaintances by—

I bleat with new acquaintances by—

I roar at work by—

I bleat at work by—

Roaring or Bleating?
Matching beliefs with behavior

This week take the time to reflect on your outward behavior. Record as many instances as you can when you didn't live out your inward beliefs—when you were a bleating sheep. Then record what you could have done differently.

The goal isn't to get discouraged—everyone has room for improvement. But instead use this as an opportunity to see where and how you can grow. And don't worry—you'll get a chance to record all the times you were a roaring lamb later on.

Be sure to bring this sheet to your next meeting.

This week my inward beliefs didn't match up with my outward behavior when—	I could have acted differently by—

26

Welcome to the Ghetto
Fighting the battle of Jericho

The Big Question [to pose for your students later in the session]

If you live behind the walls of a Christian ghetto, how do you go about moving outside of them?

You might remember singing the old gospel song, "Joshua Fit [read, Fought] the Battle of Jericho." As a kid you may have marched around your Sunday school classroom over and over singing at the top of your lungs, acting out the parts lustily, banging on drums, blowing into toy trumpets. And at just the right moment, the whole class would collapse onto the floor in a big heap of childhood energy.

Those were the days.

Here's the thing about Jericho—yes, the walls were strong and thick. Yes, the walls were tall and inhibiting. And yes, the walls seemed indestructible. With God's power, though, they came down— *but only after the Israelites realized they needed to come down.*

What if the Israelites had never acknowledged the presence of Jericho's

> "We (the church) have created a phenomenal subculture with our own media, entertainment, educational system, and political hierarchy so that we have the sense that we're doing a lot. But what we've really done is create a ghetto that is easily dismissed by the rest of society."
> Bob Briner, *Roaring Lambs: A Gentle Plan to Radically Change Your World* (Zondervan, 1993).

walls? Or what if they'd acknowledged them but then said, "Good thing those walls are there so we don't have to look at all the nasty people on the other side." Or what if they'd even gone so far as to say, "Hey, maybe we should make those walls even taller and thicker than they already are so we'll never have to worry about mixing with anyone from the other side."

It's pretty ridiculous, isn't it?

In a way that's what Christians have done in today's world. They've built walls around themselves as a way of keeping all the nasty folk out. They've said—can't listen to that music, better have our own…can't read those books, better have our own…can't look at those paintings, better have our own…and so on.

There's nothing wrong with the Christian community trying to offer alternatives to what the world offers. But too many Christians hide behind the alternatives and never mix with anyone from *the other side.* Consequently, Christians don't see the world, and even worse, the world doesn't see the Christians.

If the world doesn't see the Christians, or if all they see is a group of people who aren't willing to look beyond their own fortified walls and who want nothing to do with anyone or anything beside themselves, how will the world ever know what Christ has to offer?

The challenge is to somehow break out of what Bob Briner calls the Christian ghetto. You need to help your students realize that though there are many good things about listening to Christian music, reading Christian books and magazines, and hanging out at Christian activities, it's not good for them to live in that world exclusively. The trick is to find a healthy balance. Remember that even though Christians are not *of* the world, they still are *in* the world. Usually when that doctrine is discussed in the church, the *not of* part is empha-sized. This lesson will help you begin to emphasize the *are in* part.

Intro
So what's it like outside the sheep pen?

Give your students a chance to share the results of last session's to-do list. Then express thoughts like these—

It's important for us to recognize that sometimes—or many times—we aren't roaring lambs but bleating
sheep. The first step to impacting the world for Christ is to actually see and be aware of the world. In order to do that, we need to step out from behind our Christian walls—the Christian ghetto.

Streaming questions

Jump-start your kids' thinking with these questions. Remember, the goal is quick and lively answers.

- **Is it possible to be too involved at church?**

- **Is it wrong to give up youth group or youth camp in order to join a team or club at school?**

- **Since Jesus said Christians are *in* the world but not *of* the world, does that mean the world is a bad place?**

Listen to the music
Jars of Clay—"Headstrong"

Before you play "Headstrong," introduce it to your students by saying—

It's always dif-ficult to find balance in life. One of the things that Christians have to balance is being *in* the world without being *of* the world. Some Christians err on one side by never protecting themselves against false messages. Other

Christians err on the opposite side by never paying attention to the world at all and being ignorant of what's going on out there.

There are two problems with being out of balance. Christians who don't keep up on the world may not be prepared to fight against it, and Christians who don't show their face in the world never give nonbelievers a chance to see and hear God's truth.

Hand out **"Headstrong"** (page 36) to every student and play the song. Let them work on the activity alone, in small groups, or as a whole. Allow time for discussion if desired.

Getting into it
Life on the other side

Stuff you need
- A copy of **Life on the Other Side** for each student (page 38)
- Pens or pencils

Introduce the activity by saying something along these lines—

We're going to compare and rate pairs of activities. One activity has to do with the church world. The other relates to the outside world—the world on the other side of the Christian ghetto walls. We're not comparing the activities based on which you personally enjoy more but on which is more valuable in a general sense.

Pass out copies of **Life on the Other Side** (page 38) and pens or pencils. Students can complete this activity individually or in small groups of four or more students. After they have finished rating the activities, ask students to share some of their answers. Always have them give reasons for their choices. Remember that you are encouraging kids to think through these issues for themselves.

…or get into this
Life on the other side (same point, different spin)

Across the top of the whiteboard, write the following activities—

Stuff you need
- whiteboard and markers

- JOINING A SCHOOL SPORT
- WRITING FOR THE SCHOOL NEWSPAPER
- VISITING AN ART MUSEUM
- TAKING A FIRST-AID CLASS AT THE HOSPITAL

Feel free to add to or change the activities. The idea is to have very different activities so at least one will pique the interest of each students. Choose things that don't normally go on at church or in a youth group setting. Make sure they're all positive activities that would benefit your students in some way. Your goal is to help them see that things outside of their church subculture are not necessarily bad and, in fact, may be very good for them.

After your headings are written, continue with directions like—

As a group we're going to think about these activities and evaluate how they might be positive ways to spend our time. For example under "Joining a school sport" we may say—

- It's good physical exercise.
- It helps us learn about getting along with other people.
- It's something I enjoy and am skilled at.
- It gives me the chance to meet more kids at my school.

You may want to go one step further by saying that the only way to be involved in the listed activities is by giving up a church event now and then. Push your students to think in terms of removing their Christian ghetto walls, not just working around them.

When you're finished, ask your students these questions—

- Think of an activity outside of church that really interests you. Would you skip a Friday night lock-in to do it? If not, why? If so, do you think God minds?
- Do you think God is pleased when we get involved in positive things outside of church? Why or why not?
- Do you think there are some things that we can only get outside of our Christian ghetto (playing on a football team, visiting an art gallery)? If so is it okay to move outside of the Christian ghetto at those times, or does God want us to create our own Christian version of it?

Now pop it—
The Big Question

Through the activities in this session, you've been drawing your kids to this question, so ask it now.

If you live behind the walls of a Christian ghetto, how do you go about moving outside of them?

This question can be discussed in small groups or all together.

> "If Christian faith is ever to gain acceptance in our culture, churches and Christian colleges must do a better job of addressing the paucity of a Christian presence in American public life...Set aside all those glowing church-growth statistics and acknowledge that Christian thought and values are almost completely absent in the mainstream of American culture."
> Bob Briner, *Roaring Lambs: A Gentle Plan to Radically Change Your World* (Zondervan, 1993).

Telling stories
Sanctified Saturation

Have someone share a personal story about a time they either remained behind the walls of the Christian ghetto or stepped beyond the walls into the world. Both examples will serve your purpose.

Remember that the goal of this lesson is to encourage kids to find the balance between the positive effects of their lives in church-related activities and the negative effects of having lives that are so immersed in church-related activities that the world is shut out. The story you use should reflect that. If you don't have an appropriate story, read the following one to the group—

Dan was going to be a junior. He and his family had just moved to a new town during summer break. Dan wasn't excited about making new friends, starting at a new school, and adjusting to a new schedule. Luckily his family found a great church after being in town only a few weeks. It wasn't long before Dan was involved in youth group, the youth leadership team, and the youth worship band. Every free minute he had was spent at church. He even helped out with the VBS program in August.

When classes started in the fall, Dan was disappointed to find that almost all of his friends from youth group went to the high school on the other side of town. His family just happened to live right across the boundary line. There was one girl from his church who went to the same school, Amanda, but she was a year older and didn't go to Wednesday night youth group, so he didn't know her very well.

One of Dan's passions was drumming. His parents had bought him a new full set of Tama drums for his 16th birthday. At his old school he'd been in jazz band and a rock group that practiced on Thursday nights. It was hard for him to put it into words, but when Dan played his drums he felt free and alive—like he was really himself at those times. Plus he'd made some great friends in those groups. Most of them weren't Christians, but they had a lot of common interests and Dan felt like they respected his values.

Somehow Amanda, the girl from church, found out about his drumming skills. She played alto sax in jazz band. The drummer had graduated the year before and there was no one to replace him, at least no one who was very good. She told Dan he should try out for the group. He was interested. He talked it over with his parents who agreed he should go for it.

He auditioned the next week and was immediately accepted. The band director couldn't believe how good Dan was. Everyone in jazz band was thrilled that they were going to have such a great drummer play with them. The guitar and bass player invited Dan to stay after school and jam with them for awhile.

Dan told them he couldn't because he had youth leadership that night. "Maybe another time."

At youth leadership Dan shared about what had happened at school. He was really excited. But a few of the other members started asking him about rehearsal schedules, what the other kids were like, and

> "Everything mine is yours, and yours mine, and *my life is on display in them.* For I'm no longer going to be visible in the world; *they'll continue in the world* while I return to you."
> —Jesus, to God, talking about his followers, from John 17, *The Message*

whether he was sure it was a good idea to join.

"Sure, why not?" he said.

It turned out that jazz band had a conflicting schedule with a lot of the youth events at church. Plus two of the trumpet players were known all over town for being serious drinkers. One had gotten suspended from the cross-country team the previous spring and the other had gotten caught with alcohol in the trunk of his car at a Fourth of July party that summer.

"We're not telling you what to do," said one of the kids on the leadership team. "We just think it might be better for you to spend your time here with us instead of with them."

Dan ended up not joining jazz band. He decided maybe the kids at church were right. Maybe the best thing for him was to just avoid a bad situation. But each time he heard the jazz bland play at school, he wondered if he'd made the right choice.

Ask your teens to think about these questions—

- Was there anything wrong with the decision Dan made? Why or why not?
- What things did Dan base his decision on? Were they the right things? If not, what *should* he have based his decision on?
- When church schedules conflict with other schedules, how do you decide what to do?

Bible

Jesus liked good people and avoided bad people, right?

Read Matthew 9:9-13—the story of Jesus eating with tax

Stuff you need
- Bibles

collectors and other sinners. You may read it to your group, have students read it, or have a few people act it out while you read it. Then discuss the following questions—

- What did most people think of Matthew?
- How did Jesus treat him?
- How do you think it made Matthew feel to have Jesus treat him that way?
- How did the religious people feel about Jesus hanging out with people who were from the other side of the "church walls"?
- What if the priests had said to Jesus, "We really don't think you should be hanging out with people like that. You should stay here in the synagogue with us"?

If you think the main idea might not be clear to your teens, summarize with something like this—

Choosing to be *in* the world does not mean taking on the world's characteristic or accepting the world's beliefs. Instead it means being open to living alongside non-Christians and to getting involved in activities outside of church. Jesus didn't invite Matthew to youth group or drag him to a lock-in. He moved in Matthew's direction and entered Matthew's world. And he seemed to have a good time doing it.

To-do list
Behind and outside

Stuff you need
- A copy of Behind and Outside for each student (page 40)

Hand out a copy of **Behind and Outside** (page 40) to each student. This week they'll be keeping track of their activities *behind* the walls of the church and *outside* of it to see if they have balance in their lives. Encourage everyone to participate and remind them to bring the completed sheet to the next meeting.

Listen to the music

Headstrong
Jars of Clay

Controlled, moderate, plastic, aware and openly perfect
To know everything and not see anything

Ingest completely impressive, you wear the law as a jacket
It keeps you warm, it keeps you warm

I don't know what you've been told, but it's wrong
And I can't hold you when you fall
So headstrong. Headstrong, headstrong....

Good enough how sure a foundation
Trip on your graceful emotion
You remember it all, then cover it all

Sometimes we Christians pride ourselves on being removed from everything around us that doesn't have to do with church or youth group. We only have Christian friends. We only listen to Christian music. We avoid anyone who's a troublemaker; partier; or all-around bad person. But by avoiding all the bad stuff out there, we might be missing some of the good...assuming there is some good stuff out there.

Like the lyrics say, it's possible to "know everything (about God) and not see anything (going on in the world)." It's also possible to wear church or youth group as a jacket to keep us warm and to protect us from dealing with the world.

Think about where you fit on the line below. Mark that spot with an X

I feel that the world around me is mostly dangerous so I spend most of my time watching out for what to avoid.

●——————————————————————————————————●

I feel that the world is mostly a good place so I spend most of my time looking for stuff to jump into enthusiastically.

Depending on where you placed your X, answer one or both of the following questions—

• The reason I think the world is mostly dangerous is—

• The reason I think the world is mostly good is—

Words / Music by Dan Haseltine, Charlie Lowell, Matt Odmark, Steve Mason. © 1999 Bridgebuilding Music, Inc. / Pogostick Music; administered by Brentwood-Benson (BMI)

Life on the Other Side

Christians sometimes live in their own little world, the Christian ghetto. There may be lots of good things to enjoy in that world—but is it possible Christians may be missing something, too?

What do you think of the pairs of activities below? Is one inherently better than the other? Is one worse? What would cause you to choose one over the other?

Attending a Friday night lock-in at church.
Attending a home football game.

Being on student council.
Being in the worship band.

Attending a SADD (Students Against Drunk Driving) meeting.
Attending a youth rally with several area churches.

Going to a week of sports or music camp.
Going on a summer trip with the youth leadership team.

Going to youth group.
Going to a one-night showing of a new movie with your friends.

Being on the youth leadership team.
Being on a school athletic team.

Going to a jazz concert at a local coffeehouse.
Going to a Jars of Clay concert.

Going to a game night at church.
Going to a non-Christian friend's house to do homework.

Joining a volleyball or basketball league at church.
Joining a volleyball or basketball intramural team at school.

Reading the new issue of your favorite magazine.
Reading *Left Behind*.

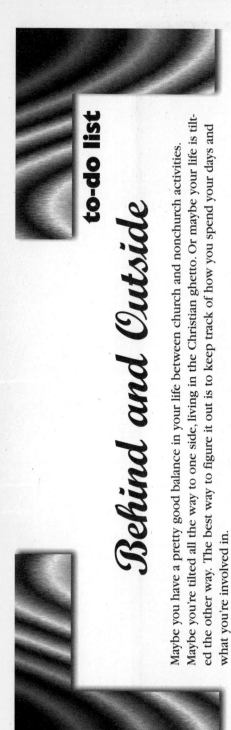

Behind and Outside

Maybe you have a pretty good balance in your life between church and nonchurch activities. Maybe you're tilted all the way to one side, living in the Christian ghetto. Or maybe your life is tilted the other way. The best way to figure it out is to keep track of how you spend your days and what you're involved in.

This week keep track of your activities *behind* the walls of the church—youth group, lock-ins, worship band practice—and *outside* of it—school play rehearsal, student council meeting, art class, football practice—to see if you have balance in your life.

Be sure to bring this sheet to your next meeting.

I was *behind* the church walls when I—

I was *outside* the church walls when I—

Think about these questions this week. You may want to jot down your thoughts.

◆ Why do I sometimes stay behind the church walls instead of going outside them?

40

◆ When I stay behind the church walls, am I trying to avoid something? If yes, what might it be?

◆ What do I like about being outside the church walls?

Jesus didn't live in a religious ghetto. He never locked himself in the temple or got overly involved in synagogue activities. To find out what he did instead, read Matthew 14:23 and Mark 1:35. Read a little bit further to see what he did next. (Whenever Jesus avoided the world it was to help prepare him to go back out into the world.)

Jesus is the perfect example of someone who broke through the walls of church and religion so he could enjoy and appreciate things on the outside and so those on the outside could enjoy and appreciate him.

Welcome to the World
You're not in Kansas anymore

The Big Question [to pose for your students later in the session]

How do Christians determine what is in the world and what is of the world? And then how do they decide what to be involved in?

For just a minute, close your eyes and think about the world. Take a good long look at it in your imagination.

It's a pretty weird and strange place, isn't it?

People run around like maniacs trying to get ahead of each other.

Celebrities stand up in front of crowds and preach about fairness and equality and goodness and then star in movies full of adultery, lying, and hate.

Politicians promise to watch out for the public's well being in exchange for votes and then promptly leave folks lying in the dust as they race off to something more important.

Advertisers tell consumers they're great, wonderful, and deserve everything they want by subtly convincing them that they're unhappy, worthless, and have no purpose until they own the right products.

> "I'm afraid many in the world view us as a flock of lambs grazing in the safe pastures surrounding our churches that have been designed to blend right in with the neighborhood landscape. We're good neighbors. We look like everyone else. And except for Sunday morning, we follow the same patterns of behavior as those who have little or no interest in religion."
> Bob Briner, *Roaring Lambs: A Gentle Plan to Radically Change Your World* (Zondervan, 1993).

Bizarre.

And dangerous.

If you really believe your students have the potential to roar like lambs and if you really believe they should be out there mixing it up with people who live on the other side of the church walls, then you'd better help them see the world clearly so they can make good decisions about how far is okay, how much is enough, and how deep is still safe.

The world has a lot to offer, but there are traps set for Christians every step of the way. Do you really think Satan is going to let a bunch of believers go traipsing around in the world without putting up a fuss? Think again.

Jesus said it clearly. Christians are

stranger and aliens in this world. They belong to another kingdom. They may be *in* the world like we talked about in the previous session, but they are not *of* the world.

What does that mean for your students? You need to point out to them that breaking down the walls of the Christian ghetto and entering the world is not the same as diving in blindly and embracing everything they come in contact with. They need to tap into God's wisdom as they try and discern what's okay and what's not.

Welcome to the world. As long as your students are careful and wise, they're in for a great ride. Otherwise, watch out.

Intro
Behind and outside, revisited

Give your students a chance to share the results of last session's to-do list. Use their responses as a springboard into this week's lesson. Clarify for students that even though you are encouraging them to move out from behind the church's walls—to break out of the Christian ghetto—you aren't encouraging them to leave God's kingdom. Rather, God's kingdom goes with them wherever they are, and even when they're in the middle of the world and their non-Christian friends they are still kingdom subjects.

Streaming questions

Jump-start your kids with these questions. Remember, the goal is quick and lively answers.

- **What things are included in a kingdom?**
- **We know God has a kingdom. How about the world? What does that kingdom look like?**
- **Can a person be part of two different kingdoms? Why or why not?**

Listen to the music
Delirious—"Touch"

As you're getting ready to play "Touch," you might want to remind your students that Christians are *in* the world but not *of* the world, as you discussed in the previous session. While it's wrong to hide from the world on the one side, it's also wrong to embrace the world's values on the other side. Entering the world is not the same as agreeing with it.

Hand out **"Touch"** (page 48) to each student and play the song for them. Let them work on the activity alone, in small groups, or as a whole. Allow time for discussion if desired.

Getting into it
Clash of the kingdoms

Divide your students into small groups of no more than three or four people. Give each group two large sheets of newsprint or two pieces of posterboard. Each group should think of themselves as an advertising firm that has been given the task of designing two posters. One will advertise the Kingdom of God and the other will advertise the Kingdom of the World. Each poster should be a hard sell for its particular kingdom and should entice people to join it.

After the groups finish have them tape their posters up for the whole group to see. Allow time for everyone to walk around the room and look at other groups' posters. Come back together and ask the following questions—

- **Which kingdom was the most attractive on the posters? Why?**
- **Which kingdom was easier to advertise? Why?**

...or get into this
In or *Of*

Start the next part of the session by mentioning these ideas—

Last time we compared activities inside the church with activities outside the church. This time we're going to compare activities that are outside the church and try to rate them as *in the world* or *of the world*. Remember that Christians are to be *in* the world but not *of* the world. This implies that things *in* the world are okay for Christians but things *of* the world are not. Let's practice making that distinction.

Give every student *In* or *Of* (page 50). They may work individually or in small groups. After everyone has finished, pull the group together and share answers.

Now pop it—
The Big Question

How do Christians determine what is in the world and what is of the world? And then how do they decide what to be involved in?

This question can be discussed in small groups or all together.

Telling stories
Close calls

Have someone share a personal story about a time when they

had to make a decision about something that is *of* the world. It doesn't matter whether they made the right or wrong decision as long as they communicate honestly and share both positive and negative consequences. Remember that the goal of this session is to illustrate that though Christians need to be out *in* the world making their presence known, they must beware of the things that are *of* the world. The story you use should reflect that. If you do not have an appropriate story, read the following one to the group—

Isabella was a member of the girl's varsity basketball team at her high

school. As a senior she was having a great year. She was a starting guard. Everything seemed to be coming together for her on the floor. All those years of summer camp and early morning practices were paying off.

In order to be on the team, Isabella had given up the teen growth group at her church. While she'd been on the junior varsity team, she'd been able to juggle both things. But when she moved to varsity, she felt like she needed to choose between the two. There just wasn't time for her to do everything and to do it well. So she chose the team. She still went to youth group on Wednesday nights and to Sunday school. She felt like staying on the team had been the right choice. She had a good shot at getting a scholarship. And she had a lot of close friendships with her teammates even though none of them were Christians.

Every Tuesday night the team ate dinner together at a different person's house. Her family had already hosted two dinners. Though she never pushed her faith on anyone, she'd prayed before the meals that were served at her home. Mostly the other girls were polite. She also noticed them watching her parents and her sisters interacting. A couple seemed surprised by the pleasant atmosphere in her home.

Several weeks into the season, Isabella was struggling in her calculus class. She was barely passing which meant she might be pulled out of Friday night's game—a home game against a team everyone wanted to beat desperately. There was going to be a quiz in Calc on Thursday. If she got an A her overall grade would be high enough to play. If she got a B she knew she'd be sitting the bench for the game.

She studied as much as she could, but it didn't seem like she had enough time to learn it all. She went in early for tutoring. She asked for help during her study hall. But by Wednesday night she was pretty worried. She'd done all she could, but she wondered whether it would be enough.

One of her teammates knew about Isabella's situation. She was pretty much in the same boat. She caught Isabella after school on Wednesday night and told her she'd managed to get the questions for the quiz. She tried giving them to Isabella, "Come on, just take them. We need you on Friday night. It you're sitting the bench, we don't stand a chance. It's only a stupid quiz, not a final. No big deal."

For a brief moment Isabella agreed. It was just a quiz. No big deal. And it wasn't like she was a bad student or had blown off the work. In fact she usually got straight A's and B's. She'd done all the studying and reviewing that any one person could do. It's not like she'd be cheating out of desperation. She

> "Stockpile treasure in heaven, where it's safe from moths and rust and burglars. It's obvious, isn't it? The place where your treasure is, is the place you will most want to be, and end up being."
> —Jesus, from Matthew 6, *The Message*

almost felt like she deserved a good grade because she'd worked so hard. Besides, the team needed her.

But Isabella said no. She realized that if she cheated, her teammates would consider her a hypocrite. At first they might be glad she could play. But what about later? Would they ever trust her again? Mostly she realized what a huge disappointment it would be to God. The price just wasn't worth it. She decided to take the quiz on her own. She felt way better about the prospect of sitting on the bench because she deserved it than she did about playing in the game if she didn't deserve to. Besides, there was always the chance that her studying would pay off and she'd get that A.

Some things to think about—

- Why did Isabella decide not to cheat?

- Do you think her teammates respected that decision or laughed at her convictions?

- In that brief moment when Isabella considered cheating, what things were going through her mind—in other words, what were the world's messages that she was struggling with?

> "Don't become so well-adjusted to your culture that you fit into it without even thinking."
> —Paul, from Romans 12, *The Message*

> ""It is my contention that the church is almost a nonentity when it comes to shaping culture."
> Bob Briner, *Roaring Lambs: A Gentle Plan to Radically Change Your World*
> (Zondervan, 1993).

Bible
The kingdom of heaven

Read Matthew 13:24-43—Jesus teaches about the kingdom of heaven. You may read it to your group or have students take turns reading it. Then discuss the following questions.

- Explain in your own words how the kingdom of God is like a tiny seed that grows.

- Explain in your own words how the kingdom of God is like yeast.

- The parable of the weeds talks about the kingdom of God and the kingdom of the world. What do you learn about each from the parable?

- What precautions should you take when you step out into the world so it doesn't exert too much control over you?

Read Luke 17:20-21 and discuss the following questions.

- How would you describe "the kingdom of God is within you" to someone who doesn't know anything about the Bible?

- How does that—or how *should* that—affect the way you live?

- Do you think people see the kingdom of God in you?

To-do list

Who's influencing whom?

Stuff you need
- A copy of Who's Influencing Whom? for each student (page 52)
- Pens or pencils

Hand out **Who's Influencing Whom?** (page 52) to your teens. Ask them to keep track of their *in's* and *of's* this week to see whether they're managing to walk *in* the world without being *of* the world—a sign of someone who is living in the kingdom of God. Remind them to bring the completed sheet to the next meeting.

Listen to the music

Touch
Delirious

I, I want to know you
And I want to show you I'm forever yours

And now, another day is dawning
Another page is turning here, for everyone to see

Yes I'm on my knees, 'cause I love you

And when you touch my life
I've been born again, I am born again
And when you touch my life
I've been born again, I am born again

I'll shine like the heavens
Shine with the words of life, light up my way

So please deliver me from walking
Beyond the truth that called me here
I'm not ashamed today

Yes, I'm on my knees, 'cause I love you

Being in the world is not the same as being of the world. Breaking out of the Christian ghetto and entering the world is not the same as embracing and agreeing with the world's messages. When someone is born again, they become part of God's kingdom and are no longer of the world even though they're still in it.

Think about when you or someone you know became a Christian. What happened on the inside?

What happened on the outside?

Try to come up with a phrase to describe what it's like to transfer from the world's kingdom to God's kingdom.

In or Of

*It's easy sometimes to recognize sin as sin. Then there are times when you stare at something—a place, a behavior, an attitude—for a long time and still wonder if it's sin, or if it's okay. Another way of putting this: is the activity you want to do (or the attitude you'd like to put on, or the person you'd like to hang with) **of** the world, or merely **in** the world? **Of** the world means that the essence or core of the activity is opposed to God's nature, and opposed to the nature he'd like you to cultivate. **In** the world means simply that the world just happens to be where a person is conducting her life and doing her best to live for God.*

So what do you think—are the items below more in the world, or of the world?

in   **of**   Watching a G-rated movie

in   **of**   Watching a PG-rated movie

in   **of**   Watching an R-rated movie

in   **of**   Attending a 2-kegger house party

in   **of**   Playing video games

in   **of**   Listening to news about a girl at school who sleeps around

in   **of**   Surfing the Net

in   **of**   Spending time in a chat room

in   **of**   Attending a concert

in   **of**   Playing a team sport

in   **of**   Going to a teen night club

in   **of**   Running for student council

in   **of**   Reading newspapers

in   **of**   Joining the school debate team

Pick one of the activities you think is **of** *the world—that is, an activity you think is inappropriate or just plain wrong for a Christian to be involved in. Do you think there are ever any exceptions—that there just might be a time when it would be fine and appropriate and not a sin for a Christian to be involved in it? Why or why not?*

Who's Influencing Whom?

Maybe you're good at being *in* the world without being of the world. Or maybe it's a struggle for you. The best way to figure out how well you're doing is to keep track of how you spend your days and what you're involved in.

Last session you compared the time you spent *behind* the church walls with the time you spent *outside* the church walls. This time, you're only going to evaluate the time you spend outside the church walls—being *in* the world and being *of* the world.

Be sure to bring this sheet to your next meeting.

The times when I was *in* the world—

The times when I was *of* the world—

Think about these questions this week. You may want to jot down your thoughts.

Jesus lived *in* the world constantly, but he never once was *of* the world. We're not perfect like Jesus was. Jesus mixed with liars, cheaters, prostitutes, and all kinds of sinners. Yet he never let their influence rub off on him. How did he manage to do that?

We're going to fail now and then when we find ourselves slipping across the line from *in* to *of*. But our goal is to keep that from happening. How can you manage to do that?

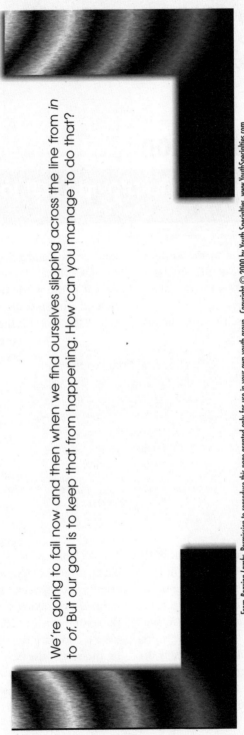

The Salt of the Earth
In praise of a high-sodium diet

The Big Question [to pose for your students later in the session]

How are you going to provide salt to those around you?

Try to imagine the world without salt. Tasteless burgers. Tasteless steaks. Heavy cookies and cakes. Blah food everywhere.

In today's world salt is used mostly for flavoring. But not long ago it was also used as a preservative. Meat was packed in salt to prevent—or at least slow down—spoiling. If you could ask your grandmother to imagine a world without salt, she'd probably think of a place full of rotten, smelly food.

Jesus called Christians the salt of the earth. He didn't mean that every now and then they should sprinkle themselves somewhere to make their presence known. He meant that they're supposed to provide flavoring and be a preservative on earth. But do they really do that? Are they out there making things more flavorful, better tasting, more lively? Are they keeping things from rotting

> "The number one way, then for Christians to be the salt Christ commands them to be is to teach His relevance, to demonstrate His relevance, to live His relevance in every area of life."
> Bob Briner, *Roaring Lambs: A Gentle Plan to Radically Change Your World* (Zondervan, 1993).

and spoiling and going to waste?

One thing's for sure. Christians can't be salt in the world if they're hiding behind church walls. And they can't be salt in the world if they don't carry their faith with them into every situation.

In *Roaring Lambs*, Briner says that the number one way for Christians to be the salt of the earth is to make Jesus relevant to those around them, to show others that Jesus has something to offer, something that they need.

It's not easy to be the salt of the earth. It means stepping out of your comfort zone, being more open and vulnerable, and taking some risks. None of those things is easy. But you don't really have a choice. Jesus didn't say, "You *can* be the salt of the earth." He didn't say, "You *have the potential* to be the salt of the earth." He didn't say, "*Consider* being the salt of the earth."

He said, "You *are* the salt of the earth."

This lesson will help your students understand what that means for their everyday lives.

Intro
Who's influencing whom?

Give your students a chance to share the results of last session's to-do list. After some students have shared, summarize with comments like these—

The reason we're supposed to be in the world is so people can see Jesus in us. Somehow we have to reflect Jesus to others, to share him with those we meet, through our words and actions. We're salt. The goal of our time together today is for us to start thinking of saltiness as making Jesus relevant to those around us.

Streaming questions

Jump-start your kids' thinking with these questions. Remember, the goal is quick and lively answers.

- **What does it mean to be the salt of the earth?**
- **What does it mean to be *relevant*?**
- **Do you think the world needs or wants the salt that Christians have?**
- **Is it possible for the world to be over-salty, meaning for Christians to do too much?**

Listen to the music
Ashley Cleveland and Michael Tait—"Salt and Light"

Tell your students that even when we understand that Jesus called Christians to be the salt of the earth we often don't know how to be salt. One thing's for sure—a Christian isn't salt by trying really, really, really hard to be really, really good.

Stuff you need
- On the *Roaring Lambs* music CD, cue up Ashley Cleveland's and Michael Tait's song "Salt and Light"
- A copy of **"Salt and Light"** for each student (page 60)
- Pens or pencils

Hand out **"Salt and Light"** (page 60) to each student and play the song. Let them work on the activity alone, in small groups, or as a whole. Allow time for discussion if desired.

Getting into it
Salt or not

After you hand out **Salt or Not** (page 62), explain that your students are

Stuff you need
- A copy of **Salt or Not** for each student (page 62)
- Pens or pencils

going to look at a list of good things that a Christian might do at school or work. Then they should rate them as being very salty, salty, or not very salty. They can complete this activity individually or in small groups.

After they're finished, ask people to share some of their answers and reasons for them. Be sure to encourage your kids to think through these issues for themselves instead of giving them "correct" answers.

...or get into this
Salt-free or high-sodium?

Divide the board into two columns. Label one SALT FREE and the other HIGH SODIUM. Then say something like this—

I want you to think about what you can offer the world. The world clearly needs the salt Christians can offer, but sometimes we don't really believe we can make a difference. In the salt-free column let's list ways the world lacks Christian influence, perhaps violence or cheating. In the high-sodium column, we might list justice and creativity.

This activity might be difficult for your students, so be sure to give them a few ideas to get their thinking started. When you've developed the lists, follow up by asking questions like these—

● Do you think Christians can make a difference in the world? Why or why not?

● What if you're trying to be salt, but you're not seeing results? Talk about that.

● Does "no results" mean you've failed? Explain your answer.

● How much time and effort do you think you need to spend in being the salt of the earth?

Now pop it—
The Big Question

Help your students focus on the main point objective of this lesson by asking—

How are you going to provide salt to those around you?

To help distinguish this questions from the others you've been discussing, you may want to have your teens discuss it in small groups.

Telling stories
Seasoning without speaking

Have someone share a personal story about a time they displayed Christian salti-

ness in the world. Remember that the goal of this lesson is to encourage kids to display their faith and make Christ relevant through the way they live and relate to others. The story you use should reflect that. If you don't have an appropriate story, read the following one to the group—

Diego has played soccer since he was about eight years old. It was one of the great passions of his life. But during all the years that he played, he never really brought any of his Christian life along with him. He practiced, he played hard, he competed. How was he any different from his teammates? He wasn't. They played just as well, if not better. And he didn't differentiate himself by having a better attitude, refraining from swearing, exhibiting better sportsmanship, or anything else. He kept his Christianity in one box and his nonchurch life in a different box. Over the years his teammates never saw anything in Diego that pointed toward Jesus.

After college Diego decided to coach a group of 12-year-old boys. He missed playing soccer, and it seemed like a great way to get back into the sport. The kids were at the age when they were beginning to *think* about the game instead of just running around and kicking the ball. Some kids were good. Others were awkward. But three times a week Diego showed up on the field to teach them to kick, pass, and shoot. More importantly he tried to teach them how to play as a team.

During college Diego had learned a lot about himself and his faith. He'd made a conscious decision to try and bring his Christianity into everything he did. He decided he'd better start living as if he believed it. He wasn't quite sure how he would accomplish that with his young soccer team.

That year they won every regular season game. For some of the kids it was their first experience on a winning team. They were proud. Through the playoffs Diego's team continued to win all the way into the finals—just one game away from being the champions. Diego knew how much it would mean to the kids to win that last game, and he did his best to help them.

But it wasn't enough. Even though they played a team they had beaten three times during the regular season, they lost the final game. The ball seemed to bounce wrong every time, and nothing seemed to click. Diego looked at their faces as they walked off the field and he could see the pain. Some of them were crying. Some were kicking the grass in anger. His heart was breaking for those kids. He didn't know what to say to them.

That afternoon they had a party at a local pizza joint. The kids seemed to have bounced back from their loss and were absorbed in the video games. Just before the party ended, one of the mothers stood up and gave Diego a present from the team. But her words were the best gift of all. "We would like to thank you for the impact you've had on our sons. Never once have we heard you say a negative word to any of the kids. You were always encouraging and always kind in what you said and how you said it. That's what brought out the best in them. Thank you."

Some of the parents and kids knew Diego was a Christian. Others didn't. Diego never preached at the kids or made them pray together before a game. All he did was teach them a little bit about how to play

> "Let me tell you why you are here. You're here to be salt-seasoning that brings out the God-flavors of this earth. If you lose your saltiness, how will people taste godliness? You've lost your usefulness and will end up in the garbage."
> —Jesus, from Matthew 5, *The Message*

soccer without yelling at them or cutting them down.

Some things to think about, some questions to explore with your group—

- How did Diego bring Jesus into his everyday life?

- Would he have been a better Christian if he'd had the team pray together before games?

- What kind of impact do you think he had on the lives of his team members?

Bible
Talk less, do more

Read Matthew 5:13-16—*The Sermon on the Mount.* You may want to read it several times in different versions to give your students more insight. Then discuss the following questions—

- What do you think Jesus was suggesting to people when he said, "You are the salt of the earth"?

- Who decides whether we're being salty or not?

- What are the criteria used to decide whether we're salty?

- Can you think of any other Bible verses or passages that might clarify our thinking about this topic? Which ones? What do they suggest?

> "Since this is the kind of life we have chosen, the life of the Spirit, let us make sure that we do not just hold it as an idea in our heads or a sentiment in our hearts, but work out its implications in every detail of our lives."
> —from Galatians 5, *The Message*

You might want to summarize for your students with these ideas—

The old saying, "Actions speak louder than words" is true. Eating lunch with outcasts at school is much saltier than telling the same people, "Jesus loves you" but then being unwilling to include them. Jesus was salty through his words but usually not until *after* he'd been salty through his actions. He loved the unlovable, touched the untouchable, and cared for the undesirables, then he preached the truth. What he *did* changed lives just as much as what he *said*.

To-do list
A highly seasoned week

Hand out copies of **A Highly Seasoned Week** (page 64) to your students. Explain by saying something like—

We're going to make a list of goals for the upcoming week about ways we can be salt. Instead of waiting for opportunities to come to us—ones we might not even recognize—we can actively be on the lookout for ways to be salt.

Remind them to bring the completed sheet to the next meeting.

Listen to the music

Salt and Light

Ashley Cleveland and Michael Tait

Salt and light, salt and light, like a city on a hill be salt and light
Who will go, who will go, plenty are called but who will go

Here I am, I will go, feet and hands, body and soul
You make an ordinary girl shine bright, in a world that needs salt and light

Fortune smiles, fortune smiles, on the land of plenty, fortune smiles
Thief at large, thief at large, stealing us blind there's a thief at large

Judgment seat, judgment seat, it makes a good recliner that judgment seat
Truth in love, truth in love, it's a powerful thing to speak the truth in love

Sometimes it's easy for Christians to sit back in their comfortable judgment seat recliners and point their fingers at all the bad stuff in the world. What's not so easy is going into the world and trying to do something about it—something more than just saying, "Hey, you need Jesus!"

Look at the lyrics. The best line is, "You make an ordinary girl shine bright." We're all ordinary. Sometimes we use that as an excuse to not do anything for God. "I'm just a nobody. What I do won't matter. Who would pay attention anyway?"

Make a list here of all the ordinary people who've affected your life for the better. Maybe they complimented you. Maybe they believed in you when no one else did. Maybe they listened when you were hurting. It might be a teacher, coach, pastor, aunt, uncle, neighbor, friend. Look at their names. Because they were willing to be salt for you, your life was changed.

Now ask yourself: Am I willing to do the same thing for someone else?

People who've affected my life	How they affected my life

Take a minute to thank God for these people. You're fortunate to have known them.

Words / Music by Ashley Cleveland, Kenny Greenberg, Michael Rhodes, Chad Cromwell. © 1999 Sole Sister Music; administered by CMI (BMI) / Songs of Windswept Pacific / Gold Club Music (BMI) / Salt Plum Music; administered by Almo Irving (ASCAP) / She Sha Music; administered by WindSwept Pacific (ASCAP)

Salt or Not

Rate each activity according to how much you think it makes a Christian a roaring lamb.

1. Doing a favor for a friend.

very salty ———————————— salty ———————————— not very salty

2. Encouraging others on your sports team.

very salty ———————————— salty ———————————— not very salty

3. Signing a drug-free pledge and sticking to it.

very salty ———————————— salty ———————————— not very salty

4. Carrying your Bible in school.

very salty ———————————— salty ———————————— not very salty

5. Helping a friend with homework.

very salty ———————————— salty ———————————— not very salty

6. Inviting a friend to your church youth group.

very salty   salty   not very salty

7. Wearing a WWJD bracelet.

very salty   salty   not very salty

8. Listening to Christian music exclusively.

very salty   salty   not very salty

9. Walking away when a sexual joke is being told.

very salty   salty   not very salty

10. Offering to partner up with the unpopular kid for a school project.

very salty   salty   not very salty

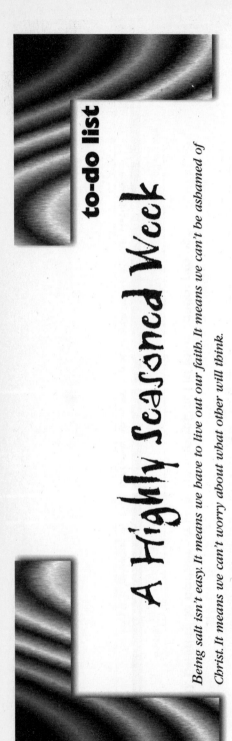

A Highly Seasoned Week

Being salt isn't easy. It means we have to live out our faith. It means we can't be ashamed of Christ. It means we can't worry about what other will think.

But it doesn't mean we can't be afraid.

Being afraid is natural. If we were never afraid, we would never have to pray and ask God for courage. Bob Briner wrote, "We have a shepherd we can trust fully, so we really ought to be out there on the front lines of battle for the cause of the Gospel."

Take some time to fill out the chart below. This is your chance to plan how you're going to go out and positively affect your world. Then watch for opportunities throughout the week to be salt.

People I want to be salt for this week—

Specific ways I can do that—

Places where I want to be salt this week—

Specific ways I can do that—

As the week goes by, record how you did. Be sure to bring this sheet to your next meeting.

Careers 101

Will the real Christian please stand up?

The Big Question [to pose for your students later in the session]

How am I going to serve Christ on the job —whatever it is?

Every person has a place in God's plan. One person's place is no more nor less important than the next—everybody's gifts are equally important to the team. Jesus' followers weren't professional preachers and pastors. They were fishermen, carpenters, and tent makers. They were ordinary folks, just like the people around them. They interacted with their neighbors. They related to their colleagues and coworkers. They were a part of the culture they lived in. And they made a difference in the world.

> "Why not believe that one day the most critically acclaimed director in Hollywood could be an active Christian layman in his church? Why not hope that the Pulitzer Prize for investigative reporting could go to a Christian journalist on the staff at a major daily newspaper? Is it really too much of a stretch to think that a major art exhibit at the Museum of Modern Art could feature the works of an artist on staff at one of our fine Christian colleges? Am I out of my mind to suggest your son or daughter could be the principle dancer for the Joffrey Ballet Company, leading weekly Bible study for other dancers in what was once considered a profession that was morally bankrupt?"
>
> Bob Briner, *Roaring Lambs: A Gentle Plan to Radically Change Your World* (Zondervan, 1993).

So where does that leave your students? Traditionally the church has communicated to Christian teens that serving God means they either become a pastor, missionary, or youth worker. Being a Christian counselor, teaching at a Christian school, or managing a Christian bookstore might qualify, too.

But Jesus was a carpenter long before he was a preacher. Don't you think he impacted his world during that time as well?

Students are done a grave disservice if they aren't encouraged to pursue careers that coincides with the way God made them. In their book, *Find Your Fit* (Bethany House, 1998) authors Jane Kise and Kevin Johnson encourage teens to examine their talents, spiritual gifts, personality type, values, and passions as they begin thinking about their futures. They contend that if teens have a good grip on who they are and how God made them all unique, they will have a much better chance of choosing a career that will satisfy and fit them. And that will result in having a positive influence on the world around them.

God didn't intend for all your students to be pastors or missionaries. But he *did* intend for all of them to be salt, to positively affect the world, and to be his disciples. Encourage your students to discover who they are and to give up the notion that only certain careers are "Christian."

Intro
A highly seasoned week in review

Give your students a chance to share the results of last session's to-do list. After your teens are finished, transition into this week's lesson with comments like—

You can be salt wherever you are, whatever you're doing. As you think about your future and your career choice, let me encourage you to explore lots of options. You'll be saltiest if you're doing what God has uniquely designed you to do, using the gifts that he's given you. You can be just as salty in the marketplace as you can behind the pulpit—maybe even more so.

Streaming questions

Jump-start your kids' thinking with these questions or others you may think of. Remember, the goal is quick and lively answers.

● **What are some "Christian" jobs?**

● **What are some "non-Christian" jobs?**

● **What determines whether a job is "Christian" or not?**

Listen to the music
Burlap to Cashmere— "Daisies and Roses"

Introduce the music to your students by saying—

Jesus has created each of you with unique characteristics. One of the things you can do to live a fulfilled life and be effective for Christ is to find a job that fits who you are. It helps to figure out what you're passionate about. We're going to listen to "Daisies and Roses" by Burlap to Cashmere. Listen for what the artists seems passionate about. Call them out as you hear them.

Hand out a copy of **"Daisies and Roses"** (page 72) to each student, and play the song. As students call out areas of passion, you can list them on the

> ## Stuff you need
> ● On the *Roaring Lambs* music CD, cue up Burlap to Cashmere's song "Daisies and Roses"
> ● A copy of **"Daisies and Roses"** (page 72)
> ● Pens or pencils
> ● Whiteboard and markers

whiteboard. Then have them work on the handout activity alone or in small groups. Allow time for discussion if desired.

Getting into it
Christian cops, coaches, & clerks

Photocopy one set of **Career Cards** (page 74) for each small group. Cut them out and place each set in a separate bag before beginning. Break into small groups of up to eight and give each group a Career Bag.

Each group member takes a card out of the bag and answers the following question by filling in the blank with what's written on their card. "HOW COULD YOU SERVE CHRIST AS A _____?"

Allow time for students to discuss their answers. Come together as a large group and ask for a representative from each small group to share key ideas from their discussion.

...or get into this
Cross careers

This activity will help your students examine how nearly any career can be worked for Christ. Pass out a copy of **Cross Careers** (page 76) to each student. Introduce the activity by saying words to this effect—

God cares more about who you are *as* you work than about what you do *for* your work. The cross on the handout is a physical symbol of how you can work at your career from a Christian perspective, no matter what it is.

Let kids work on the questions by themselves. Then break them into groups of four to six to discuss their answers.

Now pop it—
The Big Question

Bring all the kids back together to focus on the Big Question for this session—

How am I going to serve Christ while on the job—whatever career it is?

Help your teens see the similarities among the answers—some answers to the question are the same no matter what career choices they make.

Telling stories
Mechanic or minister

Have someone share a personal story about a career that is typical-

ly considered secular. The goal of this lesson is for students to see that any job can glorify God, so the story you use should reflect that. If you don't have an appropriate story, read the following one to the group—

When Isaiah was young, his mother hoped he'd go into the ministry and be a pastor or youth worker. But Isaiah didn't feel comfortable speaking in front of people. It wasn't that he wouldn't have been willing to try—he was usually pretty daring about stepping outside his comfort zone. It's just that he truly didn't sense that God wanted him to be a pastor.

On the other hand Isaiah was uncannily talented at working on machines. Even as a young kid he tinkered with things like an old toaster, a VCR, and the motor from the lawn mowers. His dad had helped him some, but it had mostly been his grandfather who'd encouraged him. He always thought that one day he'd like to be a mechanic.

As it turned out he ended up working on airplanes. He couldn't believe his good fortune at finding a job with a major airline in a nice city. Not only did he have a great home, but he had a job he loved and was good at.

In only a few years, Isaiah was promoted to supervisor. That meant it was his job to team up his employees for certain tasks. Because his real love was the hands-on work and not the organization, he always teamed himself with someone too, usually with younger and more inexperienced guys. All was fine until Eldridge was hired. In a very short amount of time, Eldridge's true self became apparent. He turned surly and disrespectful, avoided his work, and proved to be a mediocre mechanic. No one wanted to be partnered with him. Isaiah wasn't sure how the guy had ever gotten hired.

Isaiah was committed to his Christian faith and was always looking for ways to live out his faith at work. It didn't seem like there weren't many. A few guys met for a Bible study once a week. But what he really wanted to do was impact the non-Christians he worked with.

One day he realized he could impact Eldridge. Isaiah started pairing himself up with Eldridge on a regular basis. It didn't take long to realize that what Eldridge really

> "If I want to point them toward the Savior, I need to make sure my professional behavior is stellar. I need to make the best presentations, close the most successful deals, deliver the greatest product I possibly can. To them, my work is a reflection of who I am."
> Bob Briner, *Roaring Lambs: A Gentle Plan to Radically Change Your World* (Zondervan, 1993).

> "At the very least, the young people of the church should be made to see that their careers, whatever they may be, are just as vital, just as much a concern of the congregation, and just as much a part of the mission of the church as are those of the foreign missionaries the church supports."
> Bob Briner, *Roaring Lambs: A Gentle Plan to Radically Change Your World* (Zondervan, 1993).

needed more than anything else was someone to accept him and love him. That's what Isaiah set out to do. When Eldridge was disrespectful, Isaiah didn't tell him where to get off. He just kept treating him decently. When Eldridge didn't get his work done, Isaiah didn't yell at him. He just encouraged him and kept on working himself.

After several months—which felt like years to Isaiah—Eldridge started pulling his own weight. He cleaned up his language. He showed up on time. One day, out of the blue, he looked at Isaiah and said, "I don't know what it is about you, but I've never met anyone like you. You have no idea what it means to me that you haven't always been on my case. Most people just tell me what a good-for-nothing I am. I don't know what it is, but you're different from most people I know. What is it that makes you like that?"

You can guess what happened. Isaiah had a chance to share his faith with Eldridge. And all because he was a good mechanic.

Help your students think through this story with questions like these—

- What was it about Isaiah that brought salt into Eldridge's life?
- Do you think the impact he had on Eldridge is just as valuable as the impact a missionary has in another country?
- Why is Isaiah's career just as valuable as that of a pastor?

Bible
The world needs you!

Read 1 Corinthians 12:12-27—the church is one body with many parts. You can read this to your students or have students take turns reading it. You may want to use several different translations to give your students more insight into the passage. Help your student see that in the same way the church needs many different gifts, our culture at large needs many different skills to function smoothly and efficiently. Discuss questions along this line—

> "Oh yes, you shaped me first inside, then out; you formed me in my mother's womb. I thank you, High God—you're breathtaking! Body and soul, I am marvelously made! All the stages of my life were spread out before you, the days of my life all prepared before I'd even lived one day."
> —from Psalm 139, *The Message*

- What are some of the things you contribute to your church, school, job, and family?
- What skills or talents do you have that you would like to pursue further or be trained to use?
- What do you hope to contribute to society now and in the future?
- Why might someone feel that what they have to contribute isn't significant or worthwhile?

• What can you do to help encourage other Christians as they make career choices?

To-do list
Interview a roaring lamb

Stuff you need
• Copies of **Interview a Roaring Lamb** (page 78)

Hand out a copy of **Interview a Roaring Lamb** (page 78) to each student. This will be a great chance for your students to find out how people choose their careers and how they are salt while on the job, so encourage all your students to participate. Remind them to bring the completed sheet to the next meeting.

"So since we find ourselves fashioned into all these excellently formed and marvelously functioning parts in Christ's body, let's just go ahead and be what we were made to be without enviously or pridefully comparing ourselves with each other or trying to be something we aren't."
—from Romans 12, *The Message*

Listen to the music

Daisies and Roses
Burlap to Cashmere

It starts from the motions / That blade round my mind
Causes a premonition / It takes me out of time

It's a story told over / Of how I came to be
Screaming from the mountain / I was blind but now I see

I am a soldier / Trying to be one
Living in salvation / Shining like the sun

Daisies and roses / Are all I can see
All I'll ever live for / That sun, those stars, holy sea

Oh lonely soldier / Why are we alone
Thought we were all connected / My I thought we've grown

We all need attention / To heal from our cries
I dream of your smiles / To drench my dying eyes

Colors and vision / Mountains and streams
Needing each other / Oh baby it's better / Than it seems

Daisies and roses / Are all I can see
All I'll ever live for / That sun, those stars

Ten Things I Am Passionate About

The musicians seem passionate about many things. What are you passionate about? A friend? An idea? An activity? A sport? An ability? Jesus? List 10 things you are passionate about.

Words / Music by Steven Delopoulos. © 2000 Steven Delopoulos Publishing / Trippy Stick Publishing / J. Ernest Publishing (ASCAP)

Career Cards

Police officer	Athletic coach
Salesperson	Waiter

Computer programmer

Mechanic

Lawyer

Public school teacher

Cross Careers

Circle a career (listed in section 1) that interests you. Or write down one of your own choosing. Then answer the questions in sections 2-5.

3 What is one **value** a salty Christian might have who works in this career?

4 What is one **goal** a salty Christian might have who works in this career?

5 What is one **attitude** a salty Christian might have who works in this career?

2 What is one **habit** a salty Christian might have who works in this career?

police officer   writer

Web master   store manager

teacher   musician

spouse and parent   dentist

electrician   administrative assistant

physician   engineer

actor   florist

mechanic   construction worker

missionary   scientist

accountant   dancer

intelligence agent

to-do list

Interview a Roaring Lamb

This week talk to five Christians about their careers. Choose people whose job are primarily outside churches and other Christian organizations. Find out how they chose their careers and how they are able to be salt on the job.

Be sure to bring this sheet to your next meeting.

Names	Careers	Why careers were chosen	How they're salt on the job
1.			
2.			

78

3.

4.

5.

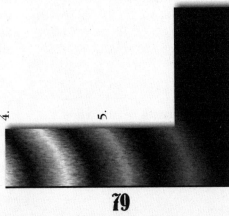

Roaring Lambs

Step up to the microphone

The Big Question [to pose for your students later in the session]

Are you ready to take your faith seriously enough to go out and be a roaring lamb in your daily world?

It's a pretty sure thing that some teens in your church are ready to roar even as you read this. Hopefully after working on these lessons they have a few ideas about how to do that. Encourage them to break out from behind the walls of the Christian ghetto by getting involved in activities they enjoy at school and reaching out to the kids who are on the fringes socially. Support their dreams about careers that fit their skills, interests, and passions where they can be the salt of the earth.

Obviously all your kids are at different places in their journeys toward becoming a roaring lamb. You'll need to deal with them at whatever places they happen to be. Begin by recognizing the positive changes already happening in their lives. Accept them where they are right now, but encourage them to move forward. Be sure your leaders and other adult mentors are helping to accomplish this.

Moving your kids toward a fully integrated Christian life is not about teaching them to preach at their friends or family. It's about teaching them to be articulate, smart, good-natured Christians who live lives consistent with their faith and the Bible. Mostly it's about sending them out to engage their culture and have a positive influence in the world.

Where are all the roaring lambs? They're right there, in your group, just waiting for their chance.

> "It is irresponsible and unscriptural for us to expect Swindoll, Dobson, and others to do our jobs for us. The call, the command to be salt, is a universal one to all Christian men and women. We can't hire anyone...to do this job for us. There are no substitutes in this game. The professionals are the coaches, and we laymen have to be the players. Their responsibility is to be sure we are equipped, that our best players get in the game at the right positions, and that there is a solid game plan."
> Bob Briner, *Roaring Lambs: A Gentle Plan to Radically Change Your World* (Zondervan, 1993).

Interview a roaring lamb revisited

Give your student's a chance to share the results of last session's to-do list. Perhaps comments like these will help you summarize—

No matter what career you decide to pursue, and no matter what you're doing in your life right now, you can be a roaring lamb. For this last lesson, you'll have the chance to dream about where you'd like to go with the information you've received over the past several weeks. Hopefully you don't want to just be a bleating sheep. Hopefully you want to break out of the Christian ghetto. Hopefully you're ready to be the salt of the earth. Hopefully you have a vision for the kind of career you'd like to pursue— or at least feel the freedom to do whatever God has gifted you for. Hopefully you want to be a roaring lamb. It's time to go for it.

Streaming questions

Jump-start your kids' thinking with some questions like these. Remember the goal is quick and lively answers.

- **When you think of a Christian spokesperson, what picture comes to mind?**
- **What goes through your mind 'when you think about being Christ's representative?**

Sixpence None the Richer— "The Ground You Shook"

Let your students have a glimpse of what's coming by telling them—

Being a roaring lamb isn't something you do alone. There are really three parts to the equation: God, the student, and other Christians. Each plays a distinct role. Let's listen to "The Ground You Shook" by Sixpence None the Richer and then we'll talk about that idea.

Stuff you need
- On the *Roaring Lambs* music CD, cue up Sixpence None the Richer's song "The Ground You Shook"
- A copy of **"The Ground You Shook"** for each student (page 84)
- Pens or pencils

Hand out **"The Ground You Shook"** (page 84) to each student and play the song. They can work alone or in small groups. Allow time for discussion if desired.

I never knew...

Before you hand out **I Never Knew...** (page 86), remind your students—

Stuff you need
- A copy of **I Never Knew...** worksheet for each student (page 86)
- Pens or pencils

Many Christians never think about the responsibility they have to speak for Jesus with their friends. They

secretly hope that someone else will do it. What they don't realize is how closely their friends watch how they live. This activity will help you understand the impact you can have on your friends. Imagine the letter we're going to read was written to you.

Pass out the letter. Have a student read it out loud while the others follow along. Students can respond by writing back on the bottom of the handout. When everyone is finished have them pair up and share what they wrote.

> "I'm calling for individual Christians to become roaring lambs—informed citizens who will enter their community dialogues on social and political issues."
> Bob Briner, *Roaring Lambs: A Gentle Plan to Radically Change Your World* (Zondervan, 1993).

this one will have the greatest impact on students if they hear a true story.

Rather than having a person share about many different experiences, ask your storyteller to relate one specific instance of being a roaring lamb. He should set the scene and tell about how he felt, what he did and said, and the results that he knows about.

If you have a student in your group who has a story to tell, choose her! It might be an event that took place prior to the beginning of this series or one that has happened since the series began—perhaps as a result of these lessons. Perhaps the ending isn't known yet.

Be sure to review with your speaker before the presentation, so the story is clear and focused.

Allow time for questions. Be prepared with some of your own.

Now pop it—
The Big Question

Through the activities in this lesson, you've been drawing your kids to this question—

Are you ready to take your faith seriously enough to go out and be a roaring lamb in your daily world?

Discuss it in small groups or all together.

Telling stories
I was a roaring lamb

Stuff you need
- A person with an appropriate story to tell (optional)

For this final session, recruit someone to tell his or her personal story about being a roaring lamb. Of all the lessons,

Bible
"Let me tell you what's gonna happen..."

Read Matthew 10:16-33—Jesus commissions the disciples. Have

Stuff you need
- Bibles

several students read it, possibly from several different versions to give your students more insight. After reading it, you may want to mention that Jesus' words still hold true for all Christians today even thought he was addressing the disciples.

Discuss these questions—

- **What's your emotional reaction to this passage?**

- **Let's list the dangers Jesus warned the disciples about.**

- **What did Jesus say to his disciples to encourage them as they faced these dangers?**

- **What dangers do you face by being a roaring lamb in your school, at work, and at home?**

- **Picture Jesus taking care of you in those places? What do you see?**

- **Are you ever ashamed or afraid to be a roaring lamb? Under what circumstances? Why?**

- **After talking about this passage, how do you feel about the prospect of being a roaring lamb?**

> "Go to the lost, confused people right here in the neighborhood. Tell them that the kingdom is here…touch the untouchable…You have been treated generously, so live generously."
> —Jesus, from Matthew 10, *The Message*

wherever they are. Ask students to write a short note to themselves on the back on their feeling about signing the covenant.

Each student should put her covenant in an envelope and address it to herself, even if it's not signed, and seal the envelope. Collect all the envelopes. Let students know you will mail the envelopes in one month—or whatever time frame you choose (and then do it at that time!).

Students will be reminded of decisions they made and encouraged to continue their roaring lamb presence. Those who don't sign now might be ready to sign when it arrives in the mail.

To-do list
Roaring Lamb Covenant

Stuff you need
- A copy of the **Roaring Lamb Covenant** for each student (page 88)
- A business-sized envelope for each student

Give each student a copy of the **Roaring Lamb Covenant** (page 88) and an envelope. Read through the covenant together. Then encourage students to sign it, but don't pressure them to do so. If they can't sign the covenant in good conscience, they should leave it blank. Reassure them that God accepts them

Listen to the music

The Ground You Shook
Sixpence None the Richer

I never knew you but you seemed to be, to me, a great man
Wise as a serpent and gentle as a hillside white lamb
We heard your voice, we saw your choice
It's written on us

I wish I'd known you and learned the way to walk the narrow path
But I am grateful that you left your words to follow like a map
Within the dark land you gave us a lamp
By which we might see

We heard your voice, we saw your choice
It's written on us

And we walk the ground that you shook
We read the words in your book
And learn how to break our own ground
All the lambs that roar beautiful sounds

Being a roaring lamb is not a solo affair. There are no lone rangers. It happens best when three different teams are present—God, you, and the church. Read the lyrics above and think about what you've learned and discussed over the past several weeks. Then make lists of how all three teams play a role in the lives of roaring lambs.

God's part	My part	The church's part

I Never Knew...

Read the following letter as though it had been written to you. (If you want, cross out the names and replace them with your name, and the name of a friend.)

Dear Friend,

Imagine my surprise when I saw you last week at the Christian concert at the convention center. During all the time we spent together at school, at my house, and just hanging out, you never once mentioned anything about Jesus. I'm a new Christian, and I wish I would have known sooner how great it could be. I wish you would have told me about the joy and strength a person has when he knows Jesus. How could you keep it to yourself? I feel like telling everyone I meet.

I hope I see you again soon. There are so many things I want to talk to you about. I'm so glad we're in the same family now!

Your new friend in Christ,

Austin

Now respond here—

Dear Austin,

Today I make a covenant with God to do my inconsistent best to be a

ROARING LAMB

I want to live out my faith everyday, everywhere,

with everyone whose life touches mine.

I can't do this myself. I need God's help and the church's encouragement.
I will pray for the strength I need. I will share my difficulties with other Christians. I will encourage other
Christians in their tough times.

I am only human and will regularly fall short of my goal. When that happens, I will not give up or forget
my commitment, but rather pick myself up, go to God for forgiveness, renew my strength, and start again
where I left off. I will do this because I know it is what God desires for me and because I trust him to be with
me every step of the way.

Signature _____

Date _____

Today I make a covenant with God to do my inconsistent best to be a

ROARING LAMB

I want to live out my faith everyday, everywhere, with everyone whose life touches mine.

I can't do this myself. I need God's help and the church's encouragement. I will pray for the strength I need. I will share my difficulties with other Christians. I will encourage other Christians in their tough times.

I am only human and will regularly fall short of my goal. When that happens, I will not give up or forget my commitment, but rather pick myself up, go to God for forgiveness, renew my strength, and start again where I left off. I will do this because I know it is what God desires for me and because I trust him to be with me every step of the way.

Signature _____ Date _____

Resources from Youth Specialties

Youth Ministry Programming

Camps, Retreats, Missions, & Service Ideas (Ideas Library)

Compassionate Kids: Practical Ways to Involve Your Students in Mission and Service

Creative Bible Lessons from the Old Testament

Creative Bible Lessons in 1 & 2 Corinthians

Creative Bible Lessons in John: Encounters with Jesus

Creative Bible Lessons in Romans: Faith on Fire!

Creative Bible Lessons on the Life of Christ

Creative Bible Lessons in Psalms

Creative Junior High Programs from A to Z, Vol. 1 (A-M)

Creative Junior High Programs from A to Z, Vol. 2 (N-Z)

Creative Meetings, Bible Lessons, & Worship Ideas (Ideas Library)

Crowd Breakers & Mixers (Ideas Library)
Downloading the Bible Leader's Guide

Drama, Skits, & Sketches (Ideas Library)

Drama, Skits, & Sketches 2 (Ideas Library)

Dramatic Pauses

Everyday Object Lessons

Games (Ideas Library)

Games 2 (Ideas Library)

Great Fundraising Ideas for Youth Groups

More Great Fundraising Ideas for Youth Groups

Great Retreats for Youth Groups

Holiday Ideas (Ideas Library)

Hot Illustrations for Youth Talks

More Hot Illustrations for Youth Talks

Still More Hot Illustrations for Youth Talks

Ideas Library on CD-ROM

Incredible Questionnaires for Youth Ministry

Junior High Game Nights

More Junior High Game Nights

Kickstarters: 101 Ingenious Intros to Just about Any Bible Lesson

Live the Life! Student Evangelism Training Kit

Memory Makers

The Next Level Leader's Guide

Play It! Over 150 Great Games for Youth Groups

Roaring Lambs

Special Events (Ideas Library)

Spontaneous Melodramas

Student Leadership Training Manual

Student Underground: An Event Curriculum on the Persecuted Church

Super Sketches for Youth Ministry

Talking the Walk

Teaching the Bible Creatively

Videos That Teach

What Would Jesus Do? Youth Leader's Kit

Wild Truth Bible Lessons

Wild Truth Bible Lessons 2

Wild Truth Bible Lessons—Pictures of God

Worship Services for Youth Groups

Professional Resources

Administration, Publicity, & Fundraising (Ideas Library)

Equipped to Serve: Volunteer Youth Worker Training Course

Help! I'm a Junior High Youth Worker!

Help! I'm a Small-Group Leader!

Help! I'm a Sunday School Teacher!

Help! I'm a Volunteer Youth Worker!

How to Expand Your Youth Ministry

How to Speak to Youth...and Keep Them Awake at the Same Time

Junior High Ministry (Updated & Expanded)

The Ministry of Nurture: A Youth Worker's Guide to Discipling Teenagers

Purpose-Driven Youth Ministry

Purpose-Driven Youth Ministry Training Kit

So *That's* Why I Keep Doing This! 52 Devotional Stories for Youth Workers

A Youth Ministry Crash Course

The Youth Worker's Handbook to Family Ministry

Discussion Starters

Discussion & Lesson Starters (Ideas Library)

Discussion & Lesson Starters 2 (Ideas Library)

EdgeTV

Get 'Em Talking

Keep 'Em Talking!

High School TalkSheets

More High School TalkSheets

High School TalkSheets: Psalms and Proverbs

Junior High TalkSheets

More Junior High TalkSheets

Junior High TalkSheets: Psalms and Proverbs

Real Kids: Short Cuts

Real Kids: The Real Deal—on Friendship, Loneliness, Racism, & Suicide

Real Kids: The Real Deal—on Sexual Choices, Family Matters, & Loss

Real Kids: The Real Deal—on Stressing Out, Addictive Behavior, Great Comebacks, & Violence

Real Kids: Word on the Street

Unfinished Sentences: 450 Tantalizing Statement-Starters to Get Teenagers Talking & Thinking

What If...? 450 Thought-Provoking Questions to Get Teenagers Talking, Laughing, and Thinking

Would You Rather...? 465 Provocative Questions to Get Teenagers Talking

Have You Ever...? 450 Intriguing Questions Guaranteed to Get Teenagers Talking

Art Source Clip Art

Stark Raving Clip Art (print)

Youth Group Activities (print)

Symbols, Phrases, and Oddities (print)

Clip Art Library Version 2.0 (CD-ROM)

Digital Resources

Clip Art Library Version 2.0 (CD-ROM)

Ideas Library on CD-ROM

Videos & Video Curricula

EdgeTV

Equipped to Serve: Volunteer Youth Worker Training Course

The Heart of Youth Ministry: A Morning with Mike Yaconelli

Live the Life! Student Evangelism Training Kit

Purpose-Driven Youth Ministry Training Kit

Real Kids: Short Cuts

Real Kids: The Real Deal—on Friendship, Loneliness, Racism, & Suicide

Real Kids: The Real Deal—on Sexual Choices, Family Matters, & Loss

Real Kids: The Real Deal—on Stressing Out, Addictive Behavior, Great Comebacks, & Violence

Real Kids: Word on the Street

Student Underground: An Event Curriculum on the Persecuted Church

Understanding Your Teenager Video Curriculum

Student Resources

Downloading the Bible: A Rough Guide to the New Testament

Downloading the Bible: A Rough Guide to the Old Testament

Grow For It Journal

Grow For It Journal through the Scriptures

Spiritual Challenge Journal: The Next Level

Teen Devotional Bible

What Would Jesus Do? Spiritual Challenge Journal

Wild Truth Journal for Junior Highers

Wild Truth Journal—Pictures of God